Celebrations and Rituals

WINTER CELEBRATIONS

Cherrytree Books

Winter Celebrations

Table of Contents

Celebrations and Rituals

WINTER CELEBRATIONS

First published in the UK in 2003
by Cherrytree Books, part of the
Evans Publishing Group
2A Portman Mansions
Chiltern Street
London W1U 6NR

McRae Books:
Publishers: Anne McRae and Marco Nardi
Series Editor: Loredana Agosta
Graphic Design: Marco Nardi
Layout: Sebastiano Ranchetti
Picture Research: Helen Farrell
Cutouts: Filippo delle Monache, Alman Graphic Design
Text: Rupert Matthews, Neil Morris, Cath Senker

Illustrations: Studio Stalio (Alessandro Cantucci, Fabiano Fabbrucci, Andrea Morandi, Ivan Stalio), Paula Holguin, MM Illustrazione (Manuela Cappon), Sabrina Marconi, Antina Breithaupt

Colour Separations: Litocolor, Florence (Italy)

In the same series:
Celebrating Prophets and Gods
End-of-Life Rituals
Everyday Celebrations and Rituals
Marriage Celebrations

Borgo Santa Croce 8—Florence, Italy.
info@mcraebooks.com

British Library Cataloguing-in-Publication Data

Matthews, Rupert
Winter. - (Celebrations and rituals)
1. Winter festivals - Juvenile literature
I. Title II. Morris, Neil III. Senker, Cath
394.2'6

ISBN 184234210X

Acknowledgements:
The Publishers would like to thank the following photographers and picture libraries for the photos used in this book.
t=top; tl=top left; tc=top centre; tr=top right; c=centre; cl=centre left; cr=centre right; b= bottom; bl=bottom left; bc=bottom centre; br=bottom right
Corbis/Contrasto: 11t, 15tr, 16tr, 38b, 29tr; Lonely Planet Images: Graham Taylor 14br, Anders Blomquist 17br, Paul Beinssen 17bl, Richard I'Anson 18tr, Richard I'Anson 19tr, Richard I'Anson 19cl, Chris Barton 24bl, Jane Sweeney 25b, Cheryl Conlon 37bl, Andrew Burke 41tr, Frances Linzee Gordon 41bl, Richard I'Anson 43tr, Richard I'Anson 43cl; Marco Lanza: 14cl, 32bc; Olycom: 39tr; The Image Works: 11br, 12cl, 13tr, 13br, 26bc, 27b, 29tr, 30cl, 31tr, 31bl, 32cl, 34tr, 34cr, 35tr, 35br, 36t, 36br, 39br, 41cr, 42cr

Printed and bound in Hong Kong by C&C Offset

1 2 3 4 5 6 7 8 9 10 09 08 07 06 05 04 03

Introduction

All over the world, winter brings feast days and festivals. Some are celebrations of the season. Others are celebrations that happen to occur during the winter months. In the Northern Hemisphere, winter weather lasts from December until early March. In the Southern Hemisphere, winter weather lasts from late June to early September. In many places, such as China, Japan, the United States and Canada, snow or ice festivals are fun occasions that help people get through the long, harsh winter. In other places, such as Mongolia and India, people celebrate the end of winter and look forward to the return of the sun's warmth. Many religious feast days also occur in winter. During winter's darkest day, Christians celebrate St. Lucia, a saint associated with light. Other saints celebrated in winter include St. Nicholas, St. Joseph and St. Patrick. The Jewish feast of Hanukkah, which celebrates victory and light, the Epiphany, which commemorates an event in the life of Jesus, and Christmas, which is one of the biggest Christian festivals, are also celebrated in winter.

***An eight-branched candle-holder called a hanukkiyah, or menorah**, is lit during the Jewish festival of Hanukkah. Like many Hanukkah menorahs, this one has a ninth candle in the centre that is used to light the others.*

***The Indians of North America travelled in the deep snow wearing snowshoes** made by attaching rawhide to wooden frames, above left.*

***Children dressed up as kings** celebrate the feast of the Epiphany in Europe.*

***This gilded and jewelled icon of St. Nicholas was made in Moscow in the late 1500s.** St. Nicholas is one of the many saints celebrated during the months of winter. He is also the patron saint of Russia.*

REASONS TO CELEBRATE WINTER

ICE AND SNOW FESTIVALS
- Harbin Ice Festival, China
- Sapporo Snow Festival, Japan
- Quebec Winter Festival, Canada

THE WINTER SOLSTICE
- Dongzhi, China
- Yalda, Iran

SAINTS' DAYS
- St. Nicholas, December 6
- St. Lucia, December 13
- St. Patrick, March 17
- St. Joseph, March 19

THE END OF WINTER
- Lohri, India
- Groundhog Day, U.S.
- Tsagaan Sar, Mongolia

Dice games were popular in ancient Rome. *Public gambling became so popular that it had to be banned, but the ban was lifted during the winter Saturnalia Festival.*

Ancient Celebrations

Winter Celebrations Through History

Many of the oldest celebrations are centred on the winter solstice, which takes place on December 21 or 22 in the Northern Hemisphere, and on June 20, 21 or 22 in the southern half of the world. It is the shortest day of the year, and the weather is often cold, so perhaps people felt they needed to cheer themselves up during midwinter. Some of the customs from ancient festivals, such as the Roman Saturnalia, are followed today.

***Nut, the Egyptian sky goddess**, is covered in stars. She arches over the earth-god, her brother Geb.*

Praising Egyptian Gods

The ancient Egyptian calendar divided the year into three seasons. These were based on the annual cycle of the life-giving Nile River. The first season was akhet, the time of flood. The second was called peret, or the time for sowing crops and the third season was called shemu, the time for the summer harvest. Peret lasted from mid-November until the end of February in our calendar and included winter and the beginning of spring. During this time, there were festivals in honour of many gods. They included a special celebration of Nut, the goddess of the sky.

Greek Winter Months

Different ancient Greek states had their own names for the months. In the calendar of Athens, the month roughly equivalent to December was named Poseidon, dedicated to the god Poseidon. During this month, towns near Athens celebrated a festival called the Rural Diónysia in honour of the god Diónysus. Celebrations included the performance of plays. The following month was named Gamelion (wedding time) because it was a popular time to get married. Anthesterion (roughly February) included a three-day festival of flowers. Then came Elphebolion, which included the festival of Artemis, who was the goddess of the hunt.

Poseidon, right, *was the god of the sea and of earthquakes. The ancient Greeks sacrificed bulls in his honor.*

Clothing was relaxed during the Saturnalia festival. *People decorated their homes and enjoyed great feasts. For a while everyone was equal—and equally merry.*

Roman Saturnalia

In ancient Rome, the Saturnalia festival began on December 17. It originally lasted for two days, but was so popular that it soon went on for a week. The festival was held in honour of Saturn, the god of seeds and planting, and it began with a sacrifice at his temple. This was followed by a time of great merrymaking. Everyone gave presents, especially wax candles. Rules were relaxed, and people were even allowed to play gambling games in public. Slaves were also free to join in the fun, and sometimes they were even waited on by their masters and mistresses during Saturnalia. Each Roman household chose a pretend king to rule over the festivities.

Some slaves wore metal collars with discs around their necks. *Each disc had the name and address of their owner. However, on Saturnalia, even slaves were free to join the celebration.*

Scandinavian Yule

A winter feast called Yule, or Jol, was probably celebrated in Scandinavia well before Christianity became established there in about A.D. 1000. Some scholars suggest the word *yule* may come from Germanic tribes called Goths who used the word *qiul* or *hiul* for *wheel.* These scholars think yule refers to the annual cycle of the sun and year coming full circle in midwinter. Some people have also suggested that yule was linked to the chief Norse god, Odin. The yule log people enjoy at Christmas today may come from the custom of burning logs during the pre-Christian Scandinavian feast.

The three most important Norse gods—Odin, Thor and Frey*—are shown on this Swedish tapestry from the 1100s. Odin, the chief god in Norse mythology, was associated with war and wisdom. He was also the protector of slain heroes.*

The Far East

Winter Celebrations in China

Many people in northern China celebrate the winter solstice—the shortest day of the year—which falls on December 21 or 22. According to the belief system of yin and yang, yin is the feminine, negative and dark side of the universe. Yang represents the masculine, positive and fiery side. The traditional solstice celebration is called Dongzhi. It marks the end of the dark part of the year. In Harbin, an ice festival is held. Blocks of ice are formed into fantastic shapes for admiring visitors to see. Winter swimming is another popular Chinese custom.

A Chinese winter hat *protects a child's head from the cold, especially during the country's popular ice festivals. In parts of northern China, the daily low temperature in January averages −25 °C (−13 °F).*

Dongzhi: Chinese Winter Solstice

Dongzhi began as an agricultural festival to celebrate the end of the harvest. The word itself means arrival of winter, but it is an optimistic festival. From this day onward, the days begin to lengthen, and the yin powers of darkness start to weaken. They give way to the warmth and light of the yang powers. In ancient times, the poor found it hard to keep warm during winter. One year it was so cold, the story goes, that many in Nanyang (in Henan Province today) suffered from painful chilblains (chapped hands). The famous Chinese herbal doctor Zhang Zhongjing prepared a large cauldron with a remedy to cure them. Today, families gather to eat delicious festival foods on Dongzhi. It is also a day to honour ancestors.

This is an illustration of Zhang Zhongjing, *a famous ancient Chinese herbal doctor. Doctors today are studying some of the treatments described in his books about traditional Chinese medicine.*

At Dongzhi, families traditionally made offerings of chopsticks, *along with oranges, flowers and incense, to the household gods. They hoped this would bring good fortune and family harmony.*

Traditional Food

Chinese people often eat dumplings called jiaozi on festival days. Some people suggest that the custom of eating jiaozi on Dongzhi was in memory of doctor Zhang Zhongjing. They say hot, tasty dumplings, filled with mutton, hot pepper and health-promoting herbs helped to keep people warm and preserve their health. Another typical dish at Dongzhi family get-togethers is tang yuan, a sweet soup made with rice-flour balls. The dish is a symbol of family unity and wealth. The word *tang*, meaning soup, sounds like the Chinese word for reunion, and *yuan* means round and complete.

THE FAR EAST

The Far East is the easternmost part of Asia. Asia extends from Africa and Europe in the west to the Pacific Ocean in the east. The northernmost part of the continent is in the Arctic. In the south, Asia ends in the tropics near the equator. Traditionally, the term Far East has referred to China, Japan, North Korea, South Korea, Taiwan and eastern Siberia in Russia. Southeast Asia includes Borneo, Brunei, Cambodia, East Timor, Indonesia, Laos, Malaysia, Myanmar, the Philippines, Singapore, Thailand and Vietnam.

Swimmers climb out of the water *at the Jingdong Gorge reservoir during the annual winter swimming gala.*

Ice skating *is a popular way to exercise in the cold winter and is not quite as bracing as plunging into freezing lakes.*

Winter Swimming

Winter swimming is popular in China. Some people in Beijing, especially older men, are members of an unofficial Polar Bear Club. They brave the subzero temperatures to dive into reservoirs and lakes, which they find invigorating. When they emerge from the water, they wrap up in towels while onlookers cheer.

Harbin Ice Festival

Harbin, in northern China, is often called the Ice City. During the long, cold winters, local fishermen used to hollow out blocks of ice and put oil lamps inside them. The ice kept the chilly winter winds from blowing out the lamps. In 1963, the first official ice lantern show was organised. People made ice lanterns just as their ancestors used to do. The show was successful, and it became an annual event. Nowadays, the Harbin ice festival takes place during January and February. Talented ice sculptors from around the world create models ranging from political figures to fairy-tale characters, animals and plants.

An impressive ice sculpture at the Harbin ice festival *looks even more spectacular at night glowing with neon lights. The ice sculptors create their masterpieces using chainsaws and other ice-carving tools.*

Japanese Festivals

Japanese winter festivals are celebrations of the season more than religious occasions. They vary according to the local area and are particularly popular in the northern islands. In Hokkaido, the northernmost island, average temperatures in February range from -2°c (28°F) to -11°c (12°F). It is there in Sapporo that Japan's biggest snow festival is held. Smaller winter festivals are held throughout the region around this time. These lively festivals give people something to look forward to during the harsh winter. At the Chichibu Night Festival, the sky is lit up with lanterns. Many ablution (ritual cleansing) festivals take place during the Japanese winter. Young men, virtually naked, immerse themselves in cold water.

Everyone enjoys building snowmen *at winter festivals. In northern Japan in particular, the long winters offer plenty of opportunities for playing in the snow.*

These children are enjoying the snow at the Sapporo snow festival. *The festival began with six snow statues built by teen-agers. Now the festival involves the whole community.*

Sapporo Snow Festival

The Sapporo snow festival began in 1950, when local high school students created six snow sculptures at Odori Park. The snow sculptures at the park became so popular that the festival is held every year. Nowadays, about 2 million people attend. There are hundreds of elaborate snow statues and ice sculptures, including almost life-sized models of famous buildings, such as the Indian Taj Mahal and the Egyptian pyramids. A contest is held to judge the sculptures.

Sapporo Specialties

At Sapporo people attach snow chains—chains with spikes—to the bottom of their shoes. This stops them from slipping in the snow. To keep warm, people put a hokkailo between layers of their clothing. A hokkailo is a small, beanbag-like pouch. By shaking the contents, you start a safe chemical reaction inside that produces heat. At the festival everyone eats ramen, noodles in hot soup. The ramen comes in three flavours: salt, soy sauce and miso (soybean paste). It is easy to cook and very tasty. Wooden sculptures made by the Ainu, the indigenous people of Hokkaido, are popular souvenirs bought at Sapporo.

This is a packet of precooked ramen, *the food that is recommended for keeping warm at the Sapporo festival. Precooked ramen is also a typical souvenir brought home by tourists.*

Chichibu Night Festival

Chichibu is a city on Honshu, Japan's largest island. The Chichibu Night Festival occurs during the first week of December. Celebrated for 300 years, the festival centres on the city's main Shinto shrine. Six giant floats, each weighing about 10 tons and decorated with rows of lanterns, are carried through the streets. Lanterns light up streets, and fireworks displays make the night as bright as day. The main event takes place on December 3, when the six floats and huge ornamental umbrellas are pushed up Dangozaka Slope, accompanied by drum music.

A float decorated with lanterns *glows in front of a fireworks display in Chichibu.*

Ablution Festivals

During January, February and March, many ablution festivals take place in Japan. They are believed to purify the body and bring good health. For example, boys ages 6 to 14—dressed only in straw skirts—gather at the Yawata Shrine in the Chigawara district. They are dowsed with cold water, parade around shivering, then return to the shrine to pray for good health. There are many Naked Men festivals where young men, dressed only in loincloths, purify themselves by pouring cold water over their bodies.

A beautiful Japanese lantern *helps light up the night for the festival of Chichibu.*

During the Yaya Matsuri (Yaya Festival), at the Yawata Shrine, *official water-dowsers pour freezing cold water over the boys. The idea is that if the boys do not catch cold from doing this, then they will not catch cold at all!*

White Month in Mongolia

Tsagaan Sar (the White Month) is a celebration of the lunar new year and begins in late January or in February. The origin of the name White Month is uncertain. White is considered the colour of health and happiness. The name may also come from the white snow this time of year or the foods made of milk that are served at the festival. The whole month is special, but the main celebration is at the start of the month. Tsagaan Sar looks forward to the end of winter and is a time to strengthen family and social ties. It is a time to visit parents, no matter where they live, feast, tell humorous stories and sing.

***A ger, also called a yurt, was the traditional home used by nomadic herders** in rural areas of Mongolia. The house is made of a wooden frame covered by warm felt cloth. An outer layer of canvas, or sometimes leather, keeps it dry inside.*

BUUZ

- 1 onion, chopped
- 2 cloves of garlic, chopped
- 2 tablespoons butter
- 1 kg minced beef
- 2 teaspoons salt
- 675 g flour
- about 125 ml water
- cooking oil
- ketchup or soy sauce (optional)

Sauté the onion and garlic in the butter in a medium frying pan until opaque. Add the beef and 1 teaspoon salt and cook until lightly browned. In a bowl, mix the flour and remaining salt. Add enough water to form a smooth and elastic dough. Knead the dough for 3–4 minutes. Divide into small pieces and roll into 3½-cm diameter tubes. Cut the tubes into 4-cm lengths. Squash each tube into a circle, 8 to 10 cm across, making the outside of the circle thinner than the centre. Spoon 3 tablespoons of beef mixture onto half of each circle. Fold the other half over, pinching the edge closed, squeeze out the air and then seal the edge completely. With an adult's help, heat 2 tablespoons of oil in a wok. Fry the dumplings for 2 minutes on each side, or until golden brown and the meat is cooked. Serve with ketchup or soy sauce.

A woman fermenting horse's milk to make airag.

AIRAG IS A DRINK MADE FROM FERMENTED HORSE'S MILK. It is a popular thirst-quenching drink on festive occasions. Some of the most well-known producers of airag are found in the Middle Gobi and Arkhangai provinces. Airag is made during the summer months. As it ages, the drink's somewhat sour taste gets stronger.

Preparing for the White Month

Preparations for Tsagaan Sar start well in advance. Houses are cleaned. Several families usually gather in the eldest man's home, where they celebrate the festival. The women prepare a lavish meal. The food includes meat dumplings called buuz, lamb patties and freshly baked biscuits. Toasts are said over airag or arkhi, mild alcoholic drinks. Whether in the cities or the countryside of Mongolia, Tsagaan Sar is a time for visiting and having fun.

A Mongolian woman in traditional costume for the New Year's festival. *Headdresses like this are worn only for special occasions.*

Heralding the New Year

Traditionally, everyone wakes up early on the first day of the new year. They raise their hands in the air to greet the first sunrise. All the family members wish the oldest man in the family a happy new year. They place their palms up, and he places his palms down over them. At dinner, lamb is served, and each person drinks at least three cups of airag or arkhi.

A woman serves tasty meat dumplings*, a popular bituun treat.*

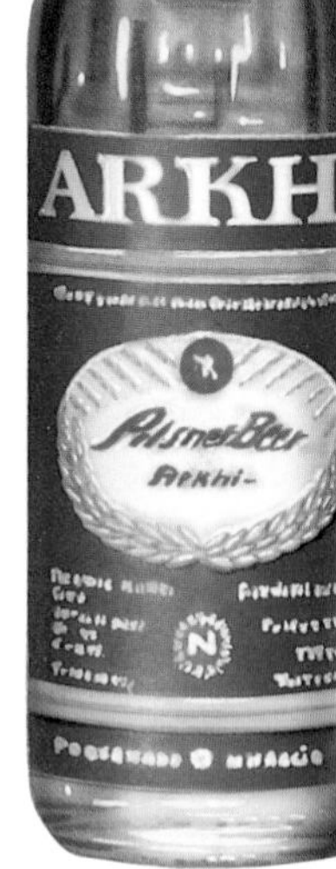

A bottle of arkhi, *a kind of mild vodka, is made from distilled horse's milk.*

Bituun

Bituun, meaning to close down, is the last dinner of the year. All the business of the year must be concluded beforehand. At the dinner table, the host slices a leg of lamb and gives everyone a piece. Then he breaks the bone and draws out the marrow. This is a symbol of the emerging new year. Then there is a long, lively dinner. Everyone must try all the dishes—milk products, meat dumplings and dessert.

Tsagaan Sar Gifts

The Mongolian people are very hospitable and often exchange gifts. Generally, visitors always bring milk or other dairy products and a few sweets for the children when they visit friends or relatives. Tsagaan Sar is a time for giving special presents. A common and symbolic gift is a khadag, which is a long piece of blue, white or yellow silk. Blue stands for eternity. White symbolises pure thoughts, and yellow represents long life and wealth. A khadag is usually presented to parents and elderly men as a mark of respect.

As a family celebrates Tsagaan Sar inside a ger, *a man plays a morin huur, a traditional two-stringed Mongolian instrument. A morin (horse) huur is traditionally topped by a carving of a horse's head.*

Agni, the ancient Hindu god of fire, *was thought to have made the sun. He acted as a messenger between gods and humans.*

Winter's End in India

The festivals of Lohri and Ganga Sagara celebrate the beginning of the end of winter. The coming warmth of the sun is represented by fire, and the fire-god Agni is especially worshipped at this time. The first such festival after the birth of a child or a wedding is seen as a particularly happy occasion for the baby or the married couple. Ceremonial offerings are made, special prayers are said, and people look forward to spring with music and dance.

This diagram shows how the Hindu calendar *approximately corresponds to the Gregorian calendar and the Indian seasons.*

COLD (winter)
FROSTY
SPRING
HOT (summer)
RAINY
AUTUMN
Pausha
Magha
Phalguna
Chaitra
Vaisakha
Jyaishta
Ashadha
Sravana
Bhadrapada
Asvina
Karttika
Magasira
January
February
March
April
May
June
July
August
September
October
November
December

Lohri

The festival of Lohri is celebrated in northwestern India, in Punjab, Haryana and other places with large Punjabi populations. The name of the festival comes from the Punjabi words *til* (meaning sesame seeds) and *rohri* (a kind of sweet brown sugar). The original tilrohri eventually became known as lohri. Both foods are thought to keep the body warm, and the festival of Lohri is associated with heat. It is celebrated on January 13 and looks forward to the end of winter.

The Hindu Calendar

The Hindu calendar has been in use in some form in India since before 1000 B.C. It is a lunar calendar, based on the month it takes for the moon to circle Earth. Twelve months make up a year of 354 days. To bring this in line with the solar year (the time it takes Earth to circle the sun), there have been adjustments and changes made to the calendar over time. The year is also divided into six seasons that correspond to the Indian climate: spring, hot, rainy, autumn, cold and frosty.

The day after Lohri, Sikhs go to the gurdwara *(temple) to celebrate the beginning of the new month. A copy of the Sikh holy book is kept beneath a canopy.*

SOUTH AND CENTRAL ASIA

South and Central Asia are areas of distinct cultures and peoples. These regions form an area at the base of Asia. Asia extends from Africa and Europe in the west to the Pacific Ocean in the east. The northernmost part of the continent is in the Arctic. In the south, Asia ends in the tropics near the equator. South Asia is made up of Afghanistan, Armenia, Bangladesh, Bhutan, India, the Maldives, Nepal, Pakistan, Sri Lanka, the Tibetan plateau in southwest China and parts of the countries of Azerbaijan and Georgia. Much of India, the largest country in south Asia, forms a peninsula that extends southward into the Indian Ocean. Central Asia includes the countries of Kazakhstan, Kyrgyzstan, Tajikistan, Turkmenistan, Uzbekistan and the West Siberian Plain.

A Celebration of Fire

The end-of-winter festival celebrates the coming of warmth, and so people naturally celebrate fire. The heat and flames of fire are associated with ancient rituals, including sacrifice. Fire also is seen as a form of communication between the gods and humans. During the Lohri festival, people build bonfires. They throw sweets, rice and sesame seeds into the flames.

During ceremonial worship called puja, *prayers are offered to Agni for a good harvest of crops.*

Candles and garlands of flowers *float on the River Ganges as offerings to Ganga.*

Celebrations in Bengal

On the island of Sagar in the Indian state of West Bengal, the end-of-winter festival is celebrated as Ganga Sagara. *Sagar* means ocean. The island is located near to where a branch from the River Ganges flows into the sea. Ganga is another name for the River Ganges, which Hindus regard as a living goddess. According to one Hindu myth, the goddess descended to Earth at the request of King Bhagiratha. People bathe in the river during the Ganga Sagara celebration.

Dance

In Punjab, festivities include the popular folk dance known as bhangra. This lively dance is well suited to winter. It ensures that everyone moves fast and keeps warm. Brightly dressed dancers move to the beat of a two-headed drum called a dholo. In some forms of the bhangra, women sing and dance.

Men dance the lively bhangra.

Bathing Festivals of India

Every year, millions of Hindus visit temples along the River Ganges and bathe in its sacred waters. One of the largest religious gatherings in the world takes place once every 12 years at the city of Allahabad. The celebration is called the Maha Khumb Mela (Great Pitcher Fair), and millions of people attend. There are many other sacred bathing sites in India, and Hindus make a pilgrimage to these on important religious dates as well.

Ganga, the Hindu river goddess, *holds a bowl and a lotus flower as she rides a legendary water monster.*

Crowds make their way to the meeting place *of two great rivers during the festival of Mauni Amavasya.*

The three most important Hindu gods *are Brahma, the creator; Vishnu, the protector; and Shiva, the destroyer.*

Mauni Amavasya

The festival of Mauni Amavasya (New Moon of the Saints) falls on the day of the new moon in the Hindu month of Magha (roughly January or February in the Gregorian calendar). On this day, Hindus flock to Allahabad, a city in northern India where two holy rivers meet—the River Yamuna and the River Ganges. At this important time, Hindus believe they are also joined by a third river, the mythical Saraswati. Hindus fast, remain silent and bathe in the holy waters.

Legendary Lesson

According to legend, a high-ranking widow and her daughter gave money to a beggar woman. The beggar told the daughter that she too would become a widow. The only way to avoid this was for someone else to fast for seven Mauni Amavasyas, and that person would become a widow instead. A milkmaid learned of this and decided to help the girl. She fasted for seven festivals, and when the high-ranking daughter married, the milkmaid's husband died. However, the god Narayan soon told the milkmaid that this had been a test, which she had passed by observing the festival correctly. For this, her husband was brought back to life.

Maha Khumb Mela

According to Hindu mythology, in ancient times the gods and demons battled over a khumb (pitcher) of amrit, a magical nectar that could provide immortality. Despite their agreement to share the amrit, the gods fled with the khumb. During the flight, which took 12 days, some amrit spilled into the River Ganges in four places—Haridwar, Nazik, Allahabad and Ujjain. The Khumb Mela takes place every three years. The fair's location rotates among the four cities, so each city hosts the festival once every 12 years, which corresponds to the 12 days of flight. The most important of the celebrations is at Allahabad. It is called the Maha Khumb Mela (Great Pitcher Fair).

During the Maha Khumb Mela, a woman prays *near one of the four places where amrit is supposed to have spilled in ancient times. Hindus believe that bathing in the Ganges at one of these four places at the time of a Kumbh Mela will give them immortality.*

Flags surround religious teachers *as they lead the festival procession.*

Processions

The important bathing festivals may include long processions. During the Maha Khumb Mela, groups of holy men, religious teachers and spiritual leaders camp near the rivers at Allahabad. Some are carried to the bathing site on trailers pulled by tractors or on top of small trucks. The vehicles are decorated with garlands of golden flowers. When they reach the sacred spot, the holy men lead the bathing.

Some sadhus have long hair and beards. *Others shave their head. They all spend a lot of time in spiritual meditation.*

SADHUS

Hindu holy men known as sadhus live a simple life full of self-discipline. They spend most of their time on their own, wandering from place to place. They have no money, and beg for only enough food to live. They carry little more than a walking stick and a bowl for begging, and some wear very few clothes. During the winter, sadhus may live alone in mountain caves, fasting for long periods of time. They live in this way in order to develop their spiritual powers. Ordinary men and women respect them for this and often turn to holy men for advice on how to lead their own lives.

This little earthenware oil lamp *is similar to those used at the time of the Maccabean Revolt.*

This statue of a Greek foot soldier, called a hoplite, *is in full military uniform, with armour and a shield. Alexander's Greek and Macedonian army had formidable strength.*

The Middle East

The Origins of Hanukkah: Festival of Lights

The Jewish calendar begins with the estimated moment of Creation. Jewish tradition places this moment a little over 3,760 years before the first year A.D. of the Gregorian calendar. The Jewish calendar is lunar, and months are alternately 29 or 30 days long. Seven times during every 19-year period, an extra 29-day month is inserted, and one of the 29-day months becomes 30 days long to keep the festivals in their season. Hanukkah is celebrated for 8 days, from the 25th of Kislev to the 3rd of Tevet. It usually falls in December, but may begin in late November. It commemorates the rededication of the Jewish Temple in 164 B.C. after the Jews recaptured Jerusalem.

Alexander the Great

The Macedonian military leader Alexander the Great was only 20 years old when his father was murdered. He took the throne, crushed his rivals and conquered the Persian Empire. The Jews, who had been ruled by the Persians, were brought under Alexander's authority about 332 B.C. Within 10 years, Alexander had created the largest empire ever known. It included Syria and Palestine in the Middle East and stretched across Asia as far as the northern provinces of India. Alexander and his successors spread Greek culture—its customs, language, money and ideas—over this vast area. The Jewish people adopted many aspects of Greek culture, such as the Greek language and clothing, but were allowed to continue to worship one God and follow their religious laws.

A scribe *is trained in preparing parchment and ink, cutting quill pens and perfecting Hebrew lettering. The Torah scrolls used today are still handwritten by a scribe.*

The Septuagint

Greek influence remained strong even after Alexander's death and the division of his empire into three main parts. One of the important new centres of power was Alexandria in Egypt. A large Greek-speaking Jewish community grew up in Alexandria. According to legend, 72 Jewish scholars translated the *Torah*, the first five books of the Hebrew Bible, into Greek in 72 days—an amazing achievement. The translation of the full Hebrew Bible took about 200 years to complete. This Greek version is known as the Septuagint. The name comes from the Latin word septuaginta, which means 70. A number of works that were included in the Septuagint but are not considered part of the Hebrew Bible are known as the Apocrypha—the "hidden" books. Among these are books called 1 Maccabees and 2 Maccabees, which tell about the reconquest of Jerusalem by the Jewish people.

THE MIDDLE EAST

The Middle East covers parts of northern Africa, southwestern Asia and southeastern Europe. Scholars disagree on which countries make up the Middle East. But many say the region consists of Bahrain, Cyprus, Egypt, Iran, Iraq, Israel, Jordan, Kuwait, Lebanon, Oman, Qatar, Saudi Arabia, Sudan, Syria, Turkey, United Arab Emirates and Yemen. The region also is the birthplace of three major religions—Judaism, Christianity and Islam.

Judah Maccabee's assault on Jerusalem *is depicted in this illustration from the 1400s.*

THE TEMPLE OF JERUSALEM

The first Jewish Temple in Jerusalem had been destroyed in 586 B.C. by the Babylonians. The Second Temple, completed in 515 B.C., was generally respected by Judaea's foreign rulers until the reign of Antiochus IV, who defiled it about 167 B.C. It is said that when the Maccabees regained control of the Temple after their revolt, they found weeds growing through the floor. The Perpetual Light, the oil lamp that they always kept burning, had gone out. The Temple was rededicated and served the community until it was destroyed once again by the Romans in A.D. 70. The only part of the Temple that survives is the Western Wall, part of the wall that enclosed the Temple courtyard. It is also called the Wailing Wall because of the sorrowful prayers said there by Jews in mourning at the loss of their beautiful Temple. It remains an important place of pilgrimage for Jewish people.

The Temple in Jerusalem, the most important Jewish religious institution in Biblical times, *is where Jews began to gather for formal prayer. After the Temple was destroyed in the 500s B.C., synagogues were built and served as Jewish houses of worship.*

The Maccabean Revolt

From 175 to 164 B.C., Antiochus IV ruled the Seleucid empire, an empire that arose in Syria after Alexander the Great's empire broke apart. Antiochus was determined to encourage Greek culture and institutions and would not allow the Jews to practise their religion freely. He set up idols of the Greek gods in all public places, and in 167 B.C. erected an altar and offered sacrifices to Zeus in the Temple of Jerusalem, which was the most holy place of the Jews. According to the Books of the Maccabees, some Jews reluctantly accepted the changes. However, others gathered forces under the leadership of Judah Maccabee. He led a revolt and conquered Judaea. In 164 B.C., the rebels retook Jerusalem, tearing down the altar to Zeus in the Temple and restoring it for their faith.

Under the rule of Antiochus IV, *it was forbidden to worship one God or to practise Jewish rites. Anyone who did would be put to death. Yet Antiochus underestimated the fighting strength of the Jews.*

The menorah in the Jews' Temple was an oil lamp with seven wicks, *like the one in this medieval picture of Moses. One wick was kept burning continually. The menorah (also called a hanukkiyah) used at Hanukkah is similar but has eight wicks, and a ninth used for lighting the others.*

Origins of the Hanukkiyah

When the Jews regained their Temple, they held festivities to rededicate the Temple to God. According to the *Talmud*, written centuries after the event, only one small jar of oil was left in the Temple, and it held only enough oil to keep the holy lamp lit for one day. But the oil miraculously lasted for eight days until more oil could be prepared. The Jewish people began to celebrate the miracle each year. People used to burn olive oil in their Hanukkah lamps, called hanukkiyahs or Hanukkah menorahs, because this was the oil used in the Temple. Nowadays, most people use candles instead on their hanukkiyah, the most common symbol of Hanukkah.

Celebrating Hanukkah

***Children are often given chocolate coins at Hanukkah.** They also may receive real money, called Hanukkah gelt in Yiddish. The money is often given in multiples of 18, because the number values traditionally assigned to each of the Hebrew letters in the word Chai (life) add up to 18.*

At Hanukkah, the Jewish people remember how the courageous Maccabees fought and beat powerful armies in the 100s B.C. to win back Jerusalem. The Maccabees regained control of the holy Jewish Temple. They cleaned and purified it, and made it fit for Jewish prayers once more. Hanukkah is not a holy day requiring fasting or prayer. It was originally a minor Jewish festival. Yet it has been celebrated for more than 2,000 years by Jewish people all over the world. Nowadays, Hanukkah is one of the most popular of all the celebrations of the Jewish calendar. The festival is based more in the home than in the synagogue, although there are special services in synagogues too.

***Doughnuts** are a popular treat enjoyed in Israel during Hanukkah.*

Celebrations in Israel

During Hanukkah, students in Israel perform plays, sing holiday songs and hold parties. Hanukkiyahs are displayed on top of important buildings, such as the Knesset (Israeli parliament). In Jewish homes, the hanukkiyah candles are lit every night and displayed in the window. Two blessings are said, one over the candles and one to remember the miracle of the oil that lasted for eight days. An extra blessing is said on the first night to express thanks for the privilege of performing the ritual. Families enjoy special foods fried in oil, especially doughnuts and potato pancakes called latkes. Children play a traditional game with a dreidel (spinning top).

***People pick wild flowers known as Blood of the Maccabees,** or cyclamen, in the hills of Judaea as Hanukkah approaches.*

Flowers in the Hills

According to the first and second books of Maccabees, several battles between the Maccabees and the Greek armies took place in the hills of Judaea (now in the West Bank). It was probably there that the Jewish leader Judah Maccabee was eventually killed during fighting in 160 B.C. Legend has it that after he was slain, white flowers speckled with blood-red dots bloomed at the very spot where he fell. These flowers are still plentiful in the area today.

Giving Cards and Gifts

Jewish people often exchange presents and send cards during Hanukkah. In some families, children are given a small gift on each night of Hanukkah, while others receive one big present on the first night. Gifts are often wrapped in blue and white wrapping paper, the colours of the Israeli flag. Jewish communities may collect gifts and money for needy families at this time of celebration.

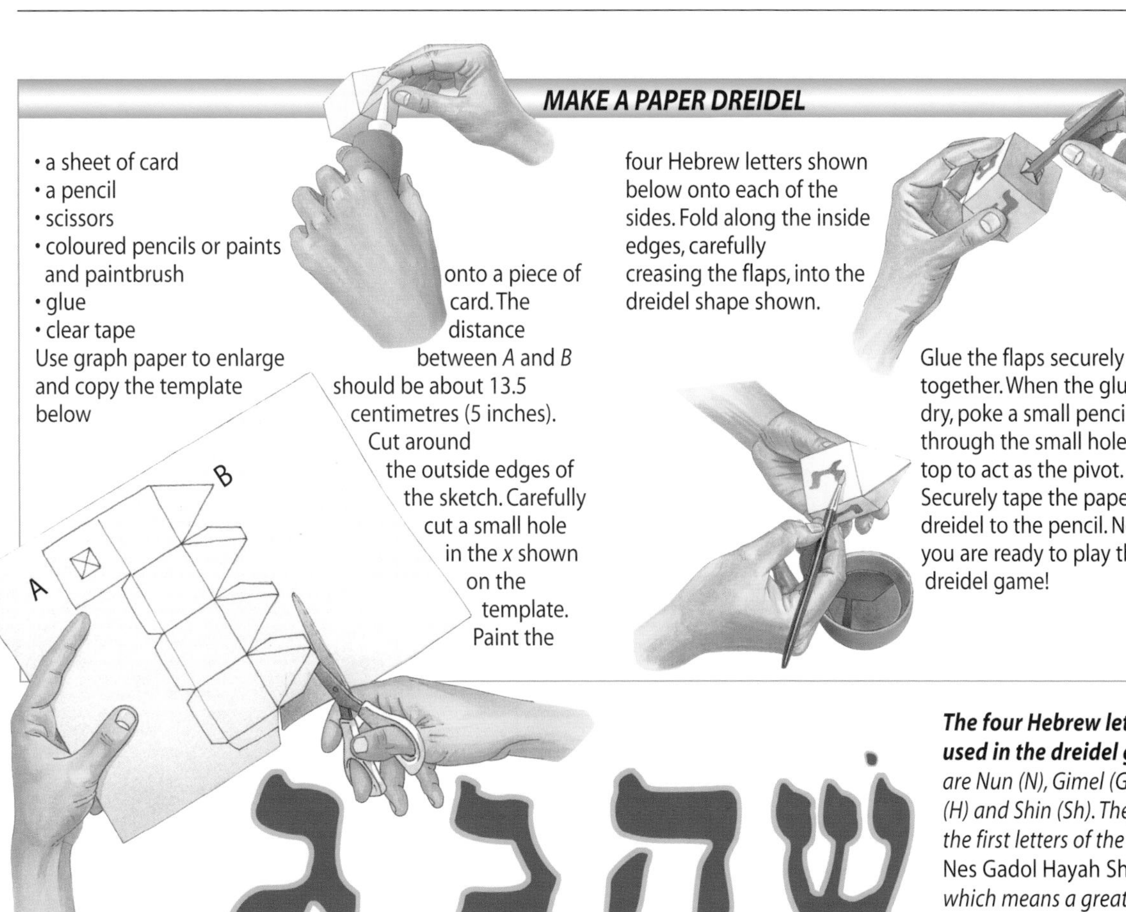

MAKE A PAPER DREIDEL

- a sheet of card
- a pencil
- scissors
- coloured pencils or paints and paintbrush
- glue
- clear tape

Use graph paper to enlarge and copy the template below onto a piece of card. The distance between *A* and *B* should be about 13.5 centimetres (5 inches). Cut around the outside edges of the sketch. Carefully cut a small hole in the *x* shown on the template. Paint the four Hebrew letters shown below onto each of the sides. Fold along the inside edges, carefully creasing the flaps, into the dreidel shape shown.

Glue the flaps securely together. When the glue is dry, poke a small pencil through the small hole on top to act as the pivot. Securely tape the paper dreidel to the pencil. Now you are ready to play the dreidel game!

ש ה נ ג

The four Hebrew letters used in the dreidel game *are Nun (N), Gimel (G), He (H) and Shin (Sh). They are the first letters of the words* Nes Gadol Hayah Sham, *which means a great miracle happened there.*

THE DREIDEL GAME
Each child starts the game with an equal number of counters or sweets (about 10) and puts one counter into a pile called the "pool." The first player spins the dreidel. If it lands on: Nun—the child does not win anything; He—he or she wins half the pool; Gimel—the child wins the pool; Shin—the child puts another counter into the pool. Whenever someone wins the pool, all the players put in one counter to start the pool again. The game ends when someone wins all the counters.

Lighting the Hanukkiyah

The hanukkiyah is an eight-branched lamp or candlestick that is central to the Hanukkah celebrations. The eight branches represent the eight days that the oil lasted when the Jews took back their Temple in 164 B.C. (see page 21). The hanukkiyah also has a ninth candle called the shamash (servant candle), which is used to light the other candles. On the first evening of the holiday, one candle is placed at the far right of the candlestick and lit using the servant candle. On the second night, two candles are placed from right to left in the spaces at the right-hand side of the hanukkiyah. They are lit from left to right. On the third night, three candles are placed, and so on until the eighth night. On the eighth and final night of the holiday, eight candles are positioned in the holder from right to left and are lit from left to right. A hanukkiyah is a treasured possession that may be handed down in a family for generations. Many different hanukkiyah designs can be found, and some families like to create their own versions.

THE HEBREW WORD *HANUKKAH* MEANS DEDICATION.
The Hebrew word has five letters, but some Hebrew letters don't sound exactly like any one English letter, so people have tried to express the sound in different ways, including Channuka, Channukah, Chanuka, Chanukah, Chanuko, Hannuka, Hannukah, Hanuka, Hanukah, Hanukkah and Kanukkah.

The candles on the hanukkiyah are lit *in a particular order. The shamash, (servant candle), is lit first and then used to light the other candles.*

Sufi and Zoroastrian Festivals

Winter festivals in the Middle East include ancient and joyous traditions. For the Muslims of the Sufi Mevlevi Brotherhood, winter brings a special occasion to praise God. The two-week long Mevlâna annual festival honours their founder, the poet Mevlâna Jalal al-Din Rumi. It is a joyous, yet solemn occasion. Yalda and Sadeh are Zoroastrian festivals still celebrated today by Zoroastrians in Iran and those from Iran living elsewhere. The Ancient Iranians divided the year into two seasons, summer and winter. According to one tradition, the winter season began in late October, and Sadeh was celebrated 100 days later. Yalda is a winter solstice festival. In ancient times, people prayed to the gods to protect their crops. Today, Zoroastrians eat fruits and nuts to celebrate the feast.

The Mevlevi Sufi Brotherhood is a Dervish order. *Members perform a whirling dance that lets them enter a trance. They believe that this dance allows them to be closer to God.*

Sufis, unlike other Muslims, use music and dance to help them reach a higher state of spirituality. *This scene from a Persian illustration of the 1500s shows Sufi musicians and dancers.*

This relief, showing a double-headed eagle, is from the old city walls of Konya.

The Mevlâna Festival, Turkey

In the city of Konya in central Turkey, members of the Mevlevi Brotherhood remember their founder Mevlâna Jalal al-Din Rumi (1207–1273). The title *Mevlâna* means our master. Mevlâna was a religious leader and poet who lived in Konya for most of his life. Mevlâna's writings address spiritual and mystical matters and are a source of inspiration for his followers. Today in Konya in early December, people begin the annual two-week Mevlâna festival. The highlight of the festival is the last day, December 17, called Sheb-i Arus, when Sufis commemorate the anniversary of his death. On this day called "nuptial night", worshippers honour Mevlâna's union with God. Pilgrims gather to witness the mysterious Sufi ritual whirling dances performed by the members of the Mevlevi Brotherhood. The dancers are accompanied by an orchestra equipped with various instruments, including pipes, drums and fiddles.

The Mevlâna Türbesi *(Tomb of Mevlâna) was built in the 1200s in Konya. A mosque, living quarters, school and tombs of other Mevlevi leaders, were also built around the mausoleum. Konya attracts many Muslim pilgrims.*

THE SASSANIAN DYNASTY

Zoroastrianism reached its height under the Sassanian Empire, which lasted from the A.D. 200s until the Muslim conquests of the 600s. The Sassanian dynasty was an ancient Iranian dynasty created by Ardashir I about A.D. 224. It was named after Sasan, one of Ardashir's ancestors. The empire Ardashir created was constantly changing in size as it competed for territory with the other powerful empires of the time, including Rome and Byzantium. Under the Sassanians, starting with Ardashir, Zoroastrianism became the official religion in Iran. The Sassanians developed impressive architecture and advanced metalwork and gem engraving. To encourage learning, scholarly works from both East and West were translated into Middle Persian, also called Pahlavi, the Sassanians' language. The Sassanian Empire was destroyed by Arab conquest in 637–651. The conquerors brought their own religion, Islam. Followers of Zoroastrianism were persecuted, and the faith almost disappeared. It was kept alive by a small number of believers, some of whom migrated to India in the 900s.

A cameo showing Shapur I, *left, battling a Roman emperor. Shapur I ruled Iran after Ardashir I, from about 240 to 270. He expanded the Sassanian Empire by fighting the Romans and taking over parts of their eastern provinces.*

Yalda

The winter solstice has been celebrated in various cultures for thousands of years. Yalda is the Zoroastrian solstice festival, held on the longest night of the year (usually December 21). The forces of evil, in the form of Angra Mainyu, are at their most powerful. The next day, which marks the start of the lengthening of daylight hours, belongs to Ahura Mazda. The solstice is celebrated as the victory of the sun over darkness and good over evil. In the past, fires were burned all night to help ensure the defeat of Angra Mainyu. There were feasts and acts of charity. Gods were honoured and prayers said to ensure the victory of the sun. Nowadays, Yalda is more a social occasion. Families enjoy dried and fresh fruits, nuts and seeds and have a good time.

Iranian women buy watermelons for the feast of Yalda. *Tradition says the melon will help people stay healthy through the winter.*

Sadeh

The word *Sadeh* means century. According to one tradition, the Sadeh festival falls on the 100th day after the beginning of winter. This puts Sadeh in late January. The name also may come from the Persian word for cold winter. Sadeh celebrates the discovery of fire as well as the defeat of the demons of winter—frost and cold. In Sassanian times, people danced around huge bonfires, and priests performed fire rituals. Wine was served and the event ended with feasts. Today in Iran, teenage boys may collect wood on the afternoon of Sadeh. People gather outside a Zoroastrian temple just before sunset to light a huge bonfire. Where there is no temple, Zoroastrians may gather inside or at home to light a fire. The celebration includes prayers from the Zoroastrians' sacred book called the *Avesta*.

A photo of a Sassanian fire temple *built on a rocky hilltop in Isfahan, Iran. At Sadeh, priests praise the discovery of fire for bringing people divine light, warmth and energy.*

St. Nicholas Day

One of the most important winter festivals in Europe is the Feast of Nicholas, also called St. Nicholas Day. St. Nicholas is a Christian saint famous for his generosity, especially to children. The festival is often organised around young people. Because St. Nicholas Day is in December, the festival is sometimes linked to the main Christian festival in that month—Christmas. Different countries celebrate the festival in various ways, but always on December 5, St. Nicholas Eve, or on December 6, the day on which St. Nicholas is thought to have died.

St. Nicholas is disguised as an old beggar in this medieval picture. *He used a disguise so that nobody would know who was bringing gifts.*

Oranges *are a traditional St. Nicholas Day treat.*

One story about St. Nicholas tells that he saved three children from a wicked murderer. *Another story says that he gave three bags of gold to three young girls so that they had enough money to marry.*

The Life of St. Nicholas

Nicholas was a Christian bishop in the Roman city of Myra (in what is now southwestern Turkey). He lived in the early A.D. 300s and was respected for his holiness. Little is known about his life, but there are many legends. One says he was imprisoned by the pagan government of the Roman Empire before Emperor Constantine the Great granted Christians the right to worship freely in 313. Another says he participated in an important Christian council at Nicaea in 325. Nicholas was wealthy, but many stories tell how he used his money to help other people, especially children.

St. Nikolaus in Germany and Austria

In the countries of Germany and Austria, St. Nicholas is called St. Nikolaus. Children receive a visit from St. Nikolaus on the night of December 5. He leaves gifts of cakes and sweets for the children to eat the next morning, St. Nikolaus Day. Children usually leave a shoe or boot beside the fireplace, so that St. Nikolaus can drop his gifts down the chimney and into them. It is said that St. Nikolaus is followed by an evil spirit who threatens to punish naughty children. Names for this spirit include Knecht Ruprecht, Hans Tripp and Krampus. Most gifts are, of course, left by the children's parents, though in some towns a man dressed as St. Nikolaus visits the children.

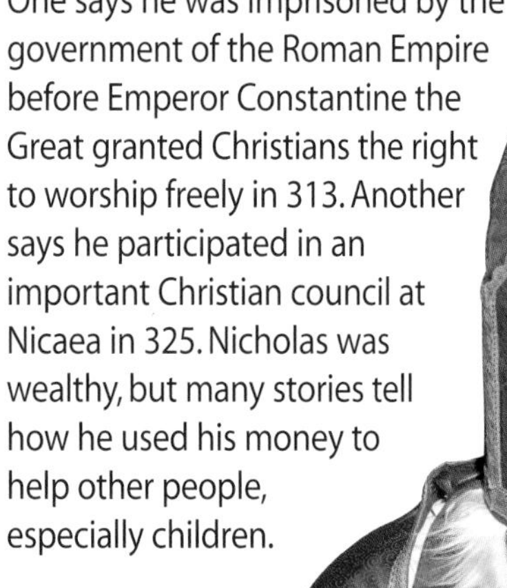

St. Nikolaus hands out sweets to good children *in Austria while his dark-faced companion, named Krampus, carries a stick to threaten naughty children.*

EUROPE

Europe is one of the smallest of the world's seven continents in area but one of the largest in population. Europe extends from the Arctic Ocean in the north to the Mediterranean Sea in the south and from the Atlantic Ocean in the west to the Ural Mountains in the east. The 47 countries of Europe include the world's largest country, Russia, as well as the world's smallest, Vatican City. Russia lies partly in Europe and partly in Asia.

The shrine of St. Nicholas is in the Basilica of San Nicola, Bari, Italy. It remains a popular site for many pilgrims.

St. Nicholas in Italy

In Italy, St. Nicholas is known as San Nicola. According to legend, merchants from Bari sailed to Myra in 1087. They went to the cathedral where the relics of St. Nicholas were kept, took the remains of the saint, and sailed back to Bari. Upon their return many people who prayed for the intercession of St. Nicholas were miraculously cured from fatal diseases. Saint Nicholas soon became popular all over Europe.

Children leave their boots or shoes out *the night of December 5 for St. Nicholas to fill with gifts.*

Sinterklaas in the Netherlands

In the Netherlands, St. Nicholas is known as Sinterklaas and is followed by a naughty imp known as Black Peter. Sinterklaas is said to arrive from Spain on a boat, then climb onto a white horse to visit the children. When children set out their shoes for gifts, they also leave behind hay or carrots for Sinterklaas's horse to eat. If they have been good children, the horse eats the food and Sinterklaas leaves sweets. But Black Peter carries a rod and threatens to shove naughty children into his sack and carry them off to Spain. Some people think that this threat may date back to the 1500s, when Spain ruled the Netherlands.

Mikulas Day in the Czech Republic and Slovakia

In Slovakia and the Czech Republic, St. Nicholas is called Mikulas. As he travels around to visit children, he journeys with an angel and a devil. Their task is to decide if a child has been good or bad in the previous year. Mikulas notes what presents the child would like to receive and hands out small sweets or cakes. The visit marks the start of the Christmas season, which lasts until January. The most important gifts arrive on Christmas Eve, December 24, but only if the angel shows that the children deserve them.

In Slovakia, children receive a small toy devil, *as well as sweets, to remind them that even good children sometimes have behaved badly.*

A group of clowns *takes part in a St. Nicholas Day parade in Amsterdam.*

St. Lucia Day

This saint's day is mainly a nonreligious celebration. St. Lucia Day is a winter festival that celebrates light at the darkest time of the year. The day is most popular in Sweden, where it is called Luciadagen (the Lucia Day). But it is also celebrated in Norway, Finland and Lucia's homeland of Italy. In America, some people of Swedish and Norwegian descent celebrate the festival as Santa (Saint) Lucia Day. The feast day of St. Lucia is on December 13, which according to the calendar at that time, was when the dark nights were at their longest.

***Candles** are used to represent the light of St. Lucia. The name* Lucia *means light.*

Lucia

Very little is known about the real Lucia, who was born in Sicily in the late 200s. According to one legend, her mother wanted her to marry a rich pagan man, but Lucia wanted to dedicate her life to Christianity, so she refused to get married. The man was so angry that he told the pagan Roman governor of Sicily that Lucia was a Christian. The governor tried to have Lucia tortured in many ways, but each time God saved her. Lucia was finally executed for being a Christian in about 304.

St. Lucia symbolises light and hope.

Patron Saint of the Blind

One legend says that one torture inflicted on St. Lucia was that her beautiful eyes were torn out. That night God gave St. Lucia new eyes that were even more beautiful than those the pagans had destroyed. Probably because of this, St. Lucia is considered the patron saint of people who are blind or who have eye problems. Every year people who suffer with their eyes gather at the church of San Geremia (Saint Jeremiah) in Venice to pray for the help of the saint. Many say the body of St. Lucia rests in this beautiful church.

***The church of San Geremia in Venice,** Italy, is where many say St. Lucia's body rests in a glass case.*

EVERYDAY LIFE FOR THE BLIND, WHO ACCORDING TO LEGEND ARE PROTECTED BY ST. LUCIA, WAS IMPROVED IN THE LATE 1820s when the Frenchman Louis Braille invented the Braille alphabet. This alphabet uses a pattern of six raised dots to represent letters or frequently used words. Blind people read Braille by rubbing their fingers across the dots.

CREATE A ST. LUCIA CROWN

- yellow card
- green card
- white card
- scissors
- a stapler
- glue

Cut a strip of yellow card 6 cm (2 1/2 inches) wide and long enough to fit around your head with an inch or two overlap to make the crown. Staple the card twice to secure the crown. Cut out seven small rectangles from the white card. Cut seven small flame shapes from yellow card. Cut several leaf shapes from green card.

Staple the flame shapes onto the white rectangles. Staple these paper "candles" to the inside of the crown at regular intervals. Then attach the leaf shapes to the crown with glue.

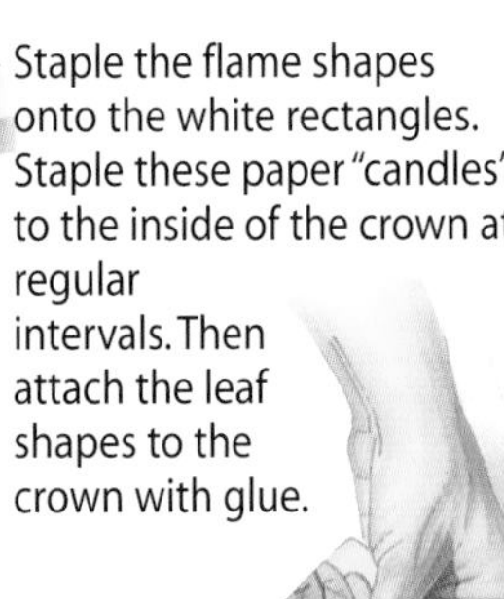

Luciadagen in Sweden

In Sweden, Luciadagen (the Lucia Day) is a popular celebration at the start of the Christmas season. Families, towns and schools celebrate the day with special costumes, foods and activities. Traditionally, the oldest daughter in the family plays the part of Lucia. She gets up early and prepares coffee. She dresses in a long white robe with a red sash and wears a crown of leaves and glowing candles on her head like a halo. She wakes the family and serves coffee and special rolls. Some cities elect a Lucia queen who visits hospitals and schools with a message of hope.

These children are making special rolls to be enjoyed on St. Lucia Day.

Lussekatter

The special rolls that are eaten on St. Lucia Day are known in Sweden as Lussekatter, which means "Lucia Cats". The buns are made with butter, milk and flour and are flavoured with saffron. Some contain raisins or other dried fruit. The traditional shape for the Lussekatter is a backward S, but they can be baked in almost any shape.

Parades

On the morning of St. Lucia Day, children hold a procession through some villages and towns. The girl chosen to be St. Lucia wears a white dress with a bright red sash around her waist. On her head, she wears a St. Lucia crown. Following her are other girls dressed in white and carrying candles or rolls. Sometimes the boys also dress in white, but they carry stars on sticks and are known as Starboys. Their job is to knock on doors so that the girls can hand out the rolls.

Schoolchildren parade through town and sing *traditional Lucia songs on St. Lucia Day.*

Epiphany Across Europe

Most Christians celebrate the Epiphany on January 6. The word *epiphany* means to make known in Greek. Among Roman Catholics and Protestants, Epiphany celebrates the day the Three Wise Men first visited the baby Jesus. The Wise Men are often referred to as kings, and the day is sometimes called Three Kings Day. In Eastern churches, the Epiphany celebrates the baptism of Jesus in the River Jordan by John the Baptist. In Italy, Spain, Latin America and much of the Caribbean, children receive gifts on this day. In France a large feast is held to mark the end of the Christmas festivities.

This illustration shows the Three Wise Men on their way to see the baby Jesus. *They are carrying gifts of gold, frankincense and myrrh to offer to the holy infant.*

In a procession of the Three Kings *in Madrid, Spain, a camel carries presents for children. In Spain, children receive their main Christmas present on January 6.*

Three Kings Day in Spain

In Spain, crowds gather to watch a procession through the streets on Three Kings Day. Huge floats carry people in fancy dress, including three men dressed as the Three Kings. At home, families share a round cake with a hole in the middle that is flavoured with almonds or candied fruit. Hidden inside is a bean or a small figure of a king or the baby Jesus. Whoever finds this treat becomes king or queen of the party. Some traditions say the finder must buy next year's cake!

GALETTE DES ROIS (KINGS' CAKE)

- 125 g butter
- 50 g granulated sugar
- 3 eggs
- 50 g ground almonds
- 2 puff pastry circles, 30-cm diameter

Preheat the oven to 200°C/400 °F/gas 6. Butter a 30-cm non-stick tin. Beat the butter and sugar with an electric mixer at high speed until creamy. Beat in two eggs, one at a time, until just blended. Stir in the almonds. Place one of the pastry circles in the prepared tin. Spoon the almond mixture onto the pastry. Beat the third egg and brush the edges of the pastry that is in the pan. Place the remaining pastry round on top and seal the edges by pinching them together. With a knife, make a few slash marks on the pastry. Brush the remaining beaten egg on top. Bake for 30 minutes or until golden brown. Serve warm.

ON THE EPIPHANY, GREEKS RECALL THE BAPTISM OF JESUS. Priests bless rivers, lakes and the sea. In some places, a cross is thrown into the water, and divers race to be the first to recover it.

This illustration shows the Three Wise Men *visiting the baby Jesus in the stable where he was born.*

The French Epiphany Feast

In France, families gather for a grand feast to celebrate the last day of Christmas. The 13 desserts of Christmas, which include fruits, nuts, sweetmeats, biscuits, cakes and pastries, form part of the meal. The Galette des Rois (King's Cake) – holds pride of place. The galette has a fève (bean) or a tiny figure of Jesus hidden inside it. The person who finds it in their slice of cake is crowned king or queen for the day and can order everyone else about!

La Befana in Italy

Children in Italy hang up their stockings on the night of January 5 in hopes that La Befana will leave them presents. La Befana is a legendary old woman. According to one story, the Three Wise Men stopped at La Befana's hut on their way to Bethlehem. They asked her to join them, but she was too busy cleaning and sweeping her house. Later she changed her mind and gathered some toys to give to the baby, but she couldn't find the holy family. Now, each year she gives presents to the good children of Italy, and lumps of "coal"—hard sugar with black food colouring—to children who are naughty!

La Befana is usually shown as a kind old woman. *Some people leave her a meal, such as sausage and broccoli for her night journey.*

This gruesome mask, typical of ones worn at Perchtenlaufen, *is enough to frighten away any witch!*

It is said that La Befana rides through the skies on a broomstick, *carrying a giant bag full of presents on her back.*

Perchtenlaufen in Austria

According to an Austrian legend, a frightening witch called Perchta roams the villages at the beginning of January. She envies happily married couples and is seen as a threat. Processions of people with giant masks parade through villages throughout the festival to chase Perchta away. Perchtenlaufen is also a seasonal festival. The masked figures chase away winter and bring blessings for the new year.

MAKE A STOCKING FOR LA BEFANA

- a large paper bag
- scissors
- a hole punch
- red ribbon
- glitter
- coloured pencils

On the flattened bag, draw a stocking shape nearly the entire size of the bag. Cut around the shape. You will now have two stocking shapes. Keeping the shapes together, punch holes at regular intervals near the edges of the paper. Do not punch holes along the top edge of the stocking. Starting with the top right edge, insert the coloured ribbon and tie a double knot to secure it. Weave in and out of the holes, finishing at the top left edge.

Knot the ribbon and then create a loop. Decorate the stocking with crayons and glitter. Hang it up and wait for La Befana to bring her gifts!

St. Patrick's Day

St. Patrick's Day is celebrated each year on March 17. St. Patrick is the patron saint of Ireland and is the most popular of the Irish saints. He is remembered as the man who brought Christianity to Ireland. Today, Irish Catholics throughout the world celebrate St. Patrick's Day. It gives people an opportunity to show their great pride in being Irish.

On the flag of Ireland, *the green represents the country's Irish Catholics, orange the Protestants and white unity.*

A shamrock is the three-leaved symbol of St. Patrick's Day. *Legend says that St. Patrick used the shamrock to teach the Christian belief in the Trinity, which says that the one God exists simultaneously as three Divine Persons—the Father, the Son and the Holy Spirit.*

St. Patrick

Patrick was born in Britain in about A.D. 390. As a young man of 16, he was captured by pirates and sold as a slave in Ireland. After six years, he escaped and returned home. Patrick became determined to convert the Irish to Christianity. He studied in France, and then returned to Ireland as a missionary in about 432. He is said to have founded about 300 churches and baptised more than 120,000 people. One of the many legends about St. Patrick tells how he rid Ireland of all its snakes by charming them into the sea, where they drowned.

St. Patrick wears bishop's vestments *in this traditional illustration.*

Celebrations

In Ireland, St. Patrick's Day is primarily a religious holiday. People honour St. Patrick by attending special religious services, enjoying family and community services and wearing shamrocks. People of Irish ancestry who live outside Ireland often celebrate the day as a nonreligious holiday. They may wear a shamrock and dress in green. Some communities stage a huge parade. Traditional Irish food and drink, such as corned beef and beer, are enjoyed, and people gather for Irish folk singing.

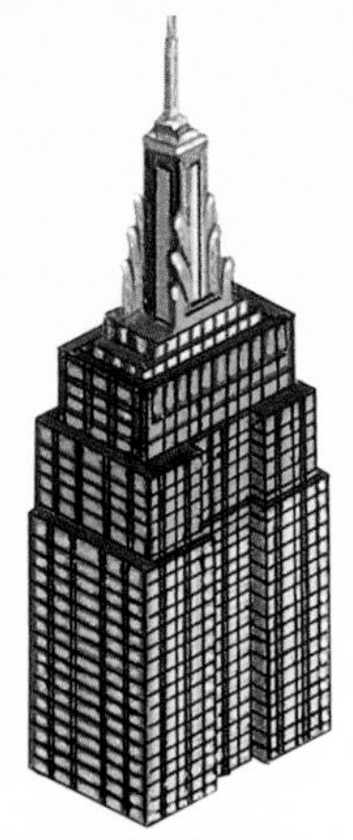

THE EMPIRE STATE BUILDING, New York, is illuminated with green lights on St. Patrick's Day. Each year the city of New York hosts the St. Patrick's Day Parade which marches down Fifth Avenue. On St. Patrick's Day Irish-Americans celebrate their heritage.

An illustration of a St. Patrick's Day hat. *Green is worn on this day because it is the colour of Ireland, the 'Emerald Isle'.*

This man is dressed for the St. Patrick's Day festivities *in New York. His face is painted the colours of the Irish flag.*

St. Joseph's Day

St. Joseph's Day is celebrated on March 19 in Italy and in countries where Italians have settled. St. Joseph is revered as the patron saint of fathers. Joseph was the husband of Mary, Jesus's mother. According to legend, in the Middle Ages a severe drought hit western Sicily. The people prayed to St. Joseph for his help. Then rain fell, and the crops grew once more. In the city of Valencia, Spain, Las Fallas de Valencia is celebrated at a similar time, from March 13 to 19.

Las Fallas de Valencia

At Las Fallas de Valencia, giant models of well-known personalities are exhibited in the streets. These fallas, also called ninots in Valencia, have been carefully crafted over the previous year. They are made of papier mâché, wood and wax. People vote for the best ninot, which is then exhibited in a museum. The high point of the festival is on St. Joseph's Day, when all the ninots—except the one voted best—are set on fire. Some people say the festival began in the Middle Ages when on the night of St. Joseph's Day, the carpenters would light a bonfire in honour of their saint. Others say that the tradition began as an ancient pagan bonfire ceremony.

An Italian father and his son, right. *At the Festa del Papà, people offer prayers to St. Joseph asking for his help in caring for their family.*

Ninots like this one are voted on during Las Fallas de Valencia. *The best of the ninots is saved, and the spectacular figure is exhibited in a museum.*

Festa del Papà, Italy

Saint Joseph is seen as the patron saint of fathers. In Italy, this saint's day is also Fathers' Day. An altar or table is decorated with candles, flowers and a statue of Joseph and Jesus. A bowl of uncooked beans symbolises the hunger of Italians in the Middle Ages and poor people today. Everyone is welcome to eat at St. Joseph's table. Here, no meat is served but there are thick vegetable soups, spaghetti sprinkled with toasted bread crumbs, various beans, pulses and breads. The bread crumbs are a reminder of Joseph the carpenter's sawdust. A special type of pastry called bignès is eaten at the festival.

St. Joseph at work as a carpenter, below. *In addition to being the patron saint of fathers, he is the patron saint of manual workers.*

American Festivals in Winter

The traditional Iroquois Midwinter Ceremony and the popular Groundhog Day are both related to the winter season. These festivals look forward to the arrival of spring. In the United States, Black History Month and Presidents' Day both fall in February. They do not relate directly to winter but rather to the birthdates of certain people important in American history.

***A popular Iroquois midwinter game required a bowl and six peach stones** or beads coloured black on one side. Players would thump the bowl on the ground and score according to how many stones came up the same colour.*

***An annual parade in celebration of Groundhog Day** features a giant groundhog float.*

Groundhog Day

People have long watched for the awakening of hibernating animals as a first sign of spring. According to one tradition, the groundhog comes out of its burrow on February 2. If the sun is shining and the animal sees its shadow, it is scared and returns to its nest. This supposedly means that winter will last for another six weeks. On a cloudy day, the groundhog won't be frightened by a shadow and will stay out to show everyone that spring is near. This tradition was originally brought to Pennsylvania by German immigrants. They had a similar belief about European badgers and hedgehogs.

***The groundhog,** sometimes called a woodchuck, is a North American burrowing rodent.*

Iroquois Midwinter Ceremony

The Iroquois traditionally held a week long festival at the time of their new year (late January or early February). Men in costume went to houses to announce the start of the ceremony. Babies born since the summer Green Corn Festival received their names during the Midwinter Ceremony. There were also sacred dances and games, speeches of Thanksgiving and feasting. During a dream-guessing ritual, the person who guessed the full meaning of someone else's dream was supposed to fulfil it.

THE AMERICAS

The continents of North America and South America make up the Western Hemisphere. North America contains Canada, Greenland, the United States, Mexico, Central America and the Caribbean Sea islands. South America contains Argentina, Bolivia, Brazil (which occupies almost half the continent), Chile, Colombia, Ecuador, Guyana, Paraguay, Peru, Suriname, Uruguay and Venezuela.

***During the first day of the Midwinter Ceremony,** Iroquois men in costumes visited each longhouse and stirred the ashes of the fires. This symbolised the scattering of the old fire of the old year and the lighting of a new fire for the new year.*

Black History Month

February is Black History Month in the United States. It honours the achievements of African Americans. Historian Carter G. Woodson started the tradition in 1926 as Negro History Week. February dates were chosen to coincide with the birthdays of two Americans who helped the lives of African Americans: Abraham Lincoln, born February 12, declared the freedom of slaves; and black leader Frederick Douglass was born February 14. The celebration was renamed Black History Month in 1976.

A young choir sings *in celebration of Black History Month.*

George Washington's *birthday has been celebrated by many people since the American War of Independence (1775-1783).*

In 1955, Rosa Parks refused to give up her bus seat to a white passenger *in Alabama. Her arrest stirred the black community and helped start the civil rights movement.*

The portraits of George Washington and Abraham Lincoln *are found on the U.S. quarter and penny.*

Presidents' Day

Presidents' Day is celebrated in the United States on the third Monday in February. It is held to honour the nation's presidents, especially George Washington, the 1st U.S. President, and Abraham Lincoln, the 16th U.S. President. Lincoln's birthday was February 12 and Washington's February 22. The third Monday always falls between these two dates and gives schools and businesses a three-day weekend.

In the side of Mount Rushmore in the Black Hills of South Dakota *are carvings of the heads of U.S. presidents George Washington, Thomas Jefferson, Abraham Lincoln and Theodore Roosevelt. More than a million people visit the granite monument each year.*

Evergreens, such as pine and fir trees, *keep their green needle-like leaves all year, even during the cold winter. At Christmas, the most popular winter festival, decorated evergreens are displayed throughout the United States, and many places in Europe.*

Snow Celebrations in the United States and Canada

Winter in the northern United States and in Canada is bitterly cold. Winter festivals brighten the coldest, darkest months of the year. Many of these festivals have historical origins and have been revived in recent times to promote local culture and to encourage tourism. Creating dramatic ice carvings and snow sculptures is common, as are sports such as skating and sledding. Warming foods are popular, including garlic and cheese, cinnamon or jam-flavoured pastries, called beavertails and maple syrup treats.

Children push their sled *down the slopes at St. Paul, Minnesota during the city's winter carnival.*

Saint Paul's Winter Carnival

The origins of this festival date to 1885, when a New York reporter wrote that the city of St. Paul, Minnesota, was too cold to live in. In response, the carnival was established to prove that the people of St. Paul were very much alive and cheerful during the winter. The events at the carnival include a parade with colourful floats, an ice-carving contest and a snow-sculpting competition. Festival badges are bought as souvenirs of this popular event.

The Quebec Winter Carnival

In the city of Quebec, the tradition of the carnival began in 1894. It was a time when people gathered for feasting and fun just before Lent. Quebec's Lenten tradition gradually died out, but the Quebec Winter Carnival was relaunched in 1955 to provide excitement and merriment during the harsh winters. Participants enjoy several traditional activities, such as canoeing in freezing conditions and dog-sled racing. There is a snow sculpture competition for which sculptors work through the night to complete their exhibits. A spectacular ice palace also is created. Parades of marching bands and floats add to the lively atmosphere.

Bread with maple syrup is prepared *at the Quebec Winter Carnival. The sweet, sticky syrup is a favourite food at the festival.*

The Voyageur Festival in Winnipeg

A huge 10-day festival celebrating the fur trade is held in Winnipeg, Manitoba, each February. More than 300 years ago, trappers and canoeists called voyageurs travelled around North America in search of fur-bearing animals. They helped develop the fur trade. Every year, they celebrated their hard work with food, drink and song. The modern version of the festival was established in 1969 to commemorate the fur traders' culture. Visitors learn how voyageurs bartered goods and sing voyageur songs. There is also arts and crafts, snow sculpting and dog-sledding races.

***Dog-sled racing** is one of the activities of the Voyageur Festival. It involves competitors from across North America.*

***The lovable ice hogs** are the mascots of Winterlude. According to legend, they arrived in Canada during the last Ice Age.*

***Some of the most popular events at Winterlude** are the outdoor performances by Canada's figure skaters.*

Winterlude and Ice Hogs in Ottawa

The Winterlude festival, in Ottawa, Canada's capital city, was established in 1979 to celebrate Canada's northern climate and culture. Thousands of artists, athletes and tourists from around the world attend. Snow sculptures are created and an ice-carving contest and sporting competitions take place. Skating on the frozen Rideau Canal is also popular. After a bracing skate, it is customary to eat deep-fried pastries called beavertails, which are flat and paddle-shaped like a beaver's tail. Magical creatures called ice hogs are the mascots of Winterlude. These legendary animals wake up from summer hibernation to enjoy the snow, ice and cold.

***Old and young enjoy skating along Ottawa's Rideau Canal Skateway.** It is the world's longest skating rink, nearly 8 kilometres (5 miles) long.*

Celebrations in Latin America

Latin America stretches from northern Mexico to southern Chile. The lands north of the equator have their winter from December to February, while those south of the equator experience winter between June and August. This means that winter festivals in Latin America can happen in different months in different countries. Whenever they take place, the festivals blend religion with fun, eating and parties.

***This vase shows the three figures that represent three of the peoples of Latin American culture**: an American Indian, a Spaniard and an African.*

Las Posadas in Mexico

On the nine evenings from December 16 until Christmas Eve, December 24, processions march through Mexican towns and villages led by dancing men in masks. The processions re-create Mary and Joseph's search for somewhere to stay as the birth of Jesus approached. Each procession stops at several houses and asks to be admitted. The householders send them away. But just as Mary and Joseph finally found lodging, so each Posadas procession eventually finds hospitality. In some areas, this is in the church, in other places a house. Food and drink are served as everyone enjoys a party. The Mexican festival of Las Posadas dates back more than 400 years to when Fra Diego de Soria began the festival in Mexico as a way of including the whole community in the celebrations of Christmas.

***Beautiful masks, like the one shown here,** are made to be worn during Las Posadas.*

***A woman carries a huge bunch of radishes** to be carved for the Noche de los Rabanos.*

Night of the Radishes in Oaxaca

One of the more unusual festivals in Latin America is the Noche de los Rabanos (Night of the Radishes), held in Oaxaca, Mexico, on December 23. The farmland of Oaxaca is fertile, but stony. The radishes grown there are very large, but have odd shapes. For years, local vegetable sellers carved the radishes into figures to display on their stalls. More than 100 years ago, this practice turned into a contest and a festival with prizes. The prize is now the central feature of a massive celebration in Oaxaca each year. The festival starts in the early evening with the judging of the radish carvings. Street parties follow and the late-night festivities end with a spectacular fireworks display.

Parintins Jungle Carnival in Brazil

In the early 1900s, two groups of travelling musicians and dancers arrived in Parintins, a small town in Brazil's Amazon rain forest. The two groups competed with each other to decide which had the better costumes, the better dancers and the better singers. Parintins's magnificent festival of Amazonian culture has grown from that chance encounter. Thousands of people flock to this isolated town from all over the Amazon to display costumes and other features of their local culture. There is dancing in the streets, and parties can last all night. The highlight remains the competition between the Garantido and the Caprichoso dance groups. Each group enacts a Boi-Bumbá, a play taken from Amazonian folklore. The play tells the story of an ox that is killed by a wicked farm manager only to be brought back to life by a local magician. The ox of each group is an elaborate creation made of wood and fabric and carried by the dancers. The main shows take place in a stadium called the Bumbódromo, which is especially constructed for Boi-Bumbá performances.

Amazonian tribesmen wear huge, colourful costumes *for the main parade of the Parintins Festival.*

An image of St. Peter *is typically carried in the procession during Brazil's Festas Juninas.*

Festas Juninas in Brazil

In Brazil, the winter falls in June, a month with so many festivals that they are collectively known as the Festas Juninas (Festivals of June). The Festival of St. Anthony of Padua takes place on June 13 and features bonfires around which people sit late into the night. For the Festival of St. John the Baptist on June 24, a bag of money or some other prize is attached to the top of a tall pole that is coated with grease. The first person to climb the pole wins the money. The Festival of St. Peter on June 29 is a more solemn occasion on which people sing hymns and pray in church.

Diá de los Tres Reyes in Mexico

In Mexico, the day the Three Wise Kings reached the baby Jesus is celebrated as the Epiphany on January 6. The day is also called Diá de los Tres Reyes (Three Kings' Day). Before this day, some children write letters to the Three Kings asking for presents. Men dressed as the Three Kings parade through towns collecting the letters. On January 5, children leave out their shoes at night to receive the gifts. On the Epiphany itself, families gather for a large meal, which traditionally includes roast pork and a special cake called a Rosca de Reyes (Kings' Ring). This is a sweet, ring-shaped bun with a tiny figure of baby Jesus inside. Whoever finds the figure in his or her slice is said to be blessed with good luck for the coming year and is obliged to invite everyone at the meal to a party on February 2.

A young girl poses with adults dressed as the Three Kings *for Mexico's Epiphany celebrations.*

This priest belongs to the Ethiopian Orthodox Church, *which has many followers in Ethiopia.*

The Nile Perch is found in many rivers in Africa. *It can grow to be more than 1.2 metres (4 feet) long and is caught for food wherever it is found.*

Dry Season in Africa

The vast continent of Africa stretches across the equator. This means that the northern areas of Africa experience winter from December to February, while those in the south experience winter from June to August. In most areas of Africa, the winter is the driest time of the year and has noticeably cooler temperatures. Only near the equator is there no change in weather in winter. The climate near the equator remains hot and moist all year. Africa is inhabited by people who follow many different religions, including traditional religions, such as Christianity and Islam.

Fishermen at the Argungu Fishing Festival *rattle stones in large gourds to herd the fish into shallow water before casting their nets.*

Africa

Argungu Fishing Festival in Nigeria

Beginning in about the 1930s, a festival celebrated the opening of most fishing seasons at Argungu on the River Sokoto in Nigeria. The festival takes place around February. It includes fishing competitions and swimming races. The highlight comes when thousands of men wade into the river, armed with nets, to catch thousands of fish for a great feast.

AFRICA

Africa lies south of Europe and west of Asia and contains 53 independent countries. Tropical rain forests dominate western and central Africa. The world's largest desert, the Sahara, stretches across northern Africa. Africa also has the world's longest river—the Nile. Much of the continent is grassland. In the north, most of the people are Arabs. The great majority of the African population lives south of the Sahara.

HARMATTAN WIND

The tropical coastlands of West Africa have a hot, wet climate. Even in winter, temperatures average more than 21 °C (70 °F). On some days, relief comes from the harmattan. This is a cool, dry wind from the northeast that blows off the Sahara when a low-pressure weather system forms in the Atlantic. The harmattan makes the weather comfortable for people unaccustomed to the stifling heat. Thus, the coming of the harmattan makes an ideal time for foreigners to take vacations in the area. Some people call the cool wind the "doctor", because it can make people feel better. However, the wind also can be very strong and often carries vast clouds of dust and sand from the desert. The dust storms can be so dense that aircraft are grounded at the airports and so strong that they can drop dust on ships many miles from the coast.

A fisherman on the River Senegal *prepares his boat for the tourists who take advantage of the harmattan.*

Sacred boxes known as tabots *are covered by ornamental cloths and parasols as they are carried in procession during the festival of Timkat.*

Timkat in Ethiopia

The great festival of Timkat (also spelled Timket) is the highlight of the religious year in Christian Ethiopia. On January 19, the festival honours the baptism of Jesus Christ by John the Baptist in the holy waters of the River Jordan. The main feature is a parade of the sacred tabot. A tabot is a wooden chest, a replica of the Ark of the Covenant, which contained the tablets carved with the Ten Commandments that God gave to Moses. A tabot is usually kept in a church where it may be seen only by the priest. At Timkat, however, the tabot is brought out of the church wrapped in cloth. Carried beneath a parasol or cloth roof, it is brought in procession to a sacred tent close to a pool of water.

A horseman in the traditional clothing of an Ethiopian warrior rides in a Timkat parade.

Timkat Festivities

The evening after the tabot is brought to the sacred tent, people pray and sing. The next morning, they gather for a religious service. The priest blesses the waters of the pool, and many people dive into the blessed waters. Then a procession of people singing and dancing in celebration bring the tabot back to the church. They prepare a celebratory meal, and the holiday continues into the following day, which is the feast of St. Michael.

A hand cross *is often carried by Ethiopian priests during the Timkat festivities.*

Winter Fun in Oceania

This wooden Maori carving is a mask of a mythological figure. *According to legend, the god Rua made the first carving.*

This carved door lintel is from the home of a Maori chief. *Maori carvings are often of ancestors.*

The thousands of islands of Oceania lie largely in tropical or sub-tropical areas. Consequently the winters are warmer than many other parts of the world. There are some changes in the weather—winter is drier than the summer in most of Oceania and cooler in the areas far enough from the equator. Traditional cultures have developed festivals for the cooler weather, and some exciting modern celebrations have been invented to take advantage of the dry conditions.

Australasia and Oceania

Maori Winter Solstice

The Maori are the native Polynesian people of New Zealand. One Maori legend said that the sky god Rangi was the father of the sun god Rua, who had two wives. In the summer, Rua lived with Hine-raumati in the south, and in winter with Hine-takurua in the north. On the day of the winter solstice, Rua left Hine-takurua to begin his journey to Hine-raumati. This was a time of rejoicing, because it meant the harvests would soon begin. People celebrated with a large fire, feasting and dancing.

A group of tribesmen dressed in traditional costumes *prepare to take part in the Great Singsing at Mount Hagen in Papua New Guinea.*

The Great Singsing in Papua New Guinea

The Great Singsing is a festival held in August at Mount Hagen in Papua New Guinea. This festival began in the mid-1900s. It was created as a way of bringing together in peace dozens of tribes from the Western Highlands to celebrate their culture of dance, song and costume. Feathers, shells, paints and mud are all used in making the dramatic costumes. Today, more than 50 tribal groups perform their singing (traditional music and dance) in a competition. Over 50,000 people flock to Mount Hagen to watch and to take part.

AUSTRALASIA AND OCEANIA

Australasia and Oceania lie east of Asia and west of the Americas. Australasia refers to Australia, New Guinea, New Zealand and other nearby islands. New Guinea and New Zealand are also considered as part of the Pacific Islands, or Oceania. Oceania is a name given to a group of many thousands of islands scattered across the Pacific Ocean. New Guinea is the largest island in the group. It contains Irian Jaya, which is a part of Indonesia, and the independent country of Papua New Guinea. Islands near the mainland of Asia (Indonesia, Japan, the Philippines) are part of Asia. Islands near North and South America (the Aleutians, the Galapagos) are grouped with those continents. Australia is itself a continent.

The Darwin Festival

In 1974, a powerful cyclone tore across northern Australia and completely flattened most of the city of Darwin, capital of the Northern Territory. A few years later, a festival was organised to celebrate the rebuilding of the city. The Darwin Festival is held every July. It celebrates the city's rich mix of cultures with concerts, plays, exhibitions and a spectacular parade. Most of the performers are local people, but artists also come from all over Oceania for this midwinter event.

***Many colourful floats** take part in the Grand Parade of the Darwin Festival in northern Australia.*

***A group of children wearing colourful headgear** wait to take part in the Grand Parade of the Darwin Festival. The Parade attracts tens of thousands of people to the city every year.*

An Australian Aborigine in a traditional costume takes part in a sacred dance.

Laura Dance and Cultural Festival

The Aborigines are the descendants of the first human inhabitants of Australia. In the 1700s, there were about 500 different tribes, each of which had its own special dances, songs and festivals. Some of these are reenacted every two years at the Laura Dance and Cultural Festival, in the town of Laura in northern Queensland. The festival is held at the Ang-gnarra Bora Ring, which has been used by local Aborigines for festivals for thousands of years. Some performers retell traditional stories through dance and song. There are also boomerang contests and displays of traditional crafts. Thousands of people visit Laura in June and camp out for the three-day festival.

Glossary

Ablution A ceremonial or religious cleansing or washing.

Altar A table or raised platform on which offerings are placed, usually found in a church, temple or other place of worship.

Ancestor A family member from a preceding generation to whom you are directly related, for example, a grandfather or great-grandfather.

Blessing Divine favour or protection. An approval or wish for happiness.

Brutal Extremely cruel or severe, causing pain and suffering.

Ceremony The celebration of an important event with an act or series of acts that follow a set of instructions established by a religion, culture or country.

Chant To sing in one tone or to repeat a prayer many times. A song or hymn used in religious ritual.

Commemorate To honour the memory of a special historical or religious event with a celebration or ceremony.

Convert To change religion or religious beliefs. To become something else.

Crop A large number of plants of any given kind that are grown for human use.

Culture A way of life. Every human society has a culture that includes its arts, beliefs, customs, institutions, inventions, language, technology and values.

Deity A god or goddess.

Devout Having strong religious beliefs.

Divine Sacred, being related to a god or goddess.

Drought A shortage of water for a long time.

Fast To choose to go without eating for a time, often for religious reasons.

Fertility The ability to produce and reproduce living things. Land is fertile when many crops can grow there.

Folklore Legends and beliefs of a group of people.

Fortune Happiness or good luck that happens in a person's life.

Harvest The reaping and gathering of grain and other food crops.

Hospitality Friendly and generous treatment of a guest or visitor.

Icon An image of a god or goddess that is considered sacred and is given special respect.

Incense A material that produces perfumed smoke when burned, usually made from plant products.

Indigenous people The original people living in a country or area before other people settled there, and their descendants.

Jews Descendants of an ancient people called the Hebrews or Israelites who practise Judaism.

Lunar calendar A calendar that marks the passing of years by following the phases of the moon. Lunar calendars are still used today by the members of some religions and cultures.

Meditate To think privately or to focus one's mind on serious or religious thoughts.

Migrate To move to a new area or country in search of work or better living conditions.

Missionary A person sent by a religious group to preach a faith and to convert others to that faith.

Monastery A place where a community of religious people, such as monks, live.

Mourning A period following a person's death during which people express deep sorrow and may perform special rituals in observance of that death.

Muslim A person who follows the religion of Islam.

Pagan A person who is not, for example, a Christian, Jew or Muslim, and who may worship many gods or no god. Modern pagans practise some forms of ancient religions.

Parasol A decorative umbrella often used as protection against sunlight.

Persecution The punishment and harassment of a person or a group of people because of their beliefs and principles, such as their religion, or because of their race or gender, or other personal characteristics.

Pilgrimage A journey taken to visit a holy place.

Procession A parade held for a religious ceremony or ritual.

Prophet A person who has been inspired by God and communicates God's will or interprets God's message to the people.

Prosperous Successful; thriving; doing well; fortunate.

Recite To say something, such as a prayer or verse, to an audience or in a group of people.

Reflection The act of careful and serious thinking.

Ritual A set of repeated actions done in a precise way, usually with a solemn meaning or significance.

Sacred Holy or precious.

Sacrifice The killing of an animal, which is offered to a god or gods as part of worship.

Saint A holy person who becomes a recognised religious hero by displaying a virtue or virtues valued by his or her religion. A patron saint is a holy person believed to protect the interests of a country, place, group, trade, profession or activity.

Slave A person who is forced to work without pay. A slave is someone who is the property of another person and has no personal rights or freedom.

Solstice One of two moments each year when the sun appears at its northernmost or southernmost position in the sky. In the Northern Hemisphere the summer solstice occurs on June 20, 21 or 22, and the winter solstice occurs on December 21 or 22. In the Southern Hemisphere the solstices are reversed.

Sow To plant or scatter seeds.

Spirit A good or bad supernatural being or force.

Symbolise To stand for or represent.

Synagogue A Jewish house of worship and a centre of Jewish education and social life.

Ten Commandments Ten rules of life given to Moses by God on Mount Sinai, which all Jews and Christians are taught to follow.

Torah The Hebrew name for the first five books of the *Bible*.

Tradition The beliefs, opinions, customs and stories passed from generation to generation by word of mouth or by practice.

Venerate To honour or to pay deep respect.

Widow A woman whose husband is dead and who has not married again. A widower is a man whose wife is dead and who has not married again.

Winter The two hemispheres have winter at different times because Earth is slightly tilted toward the sun. Winter in each hemisphere occurs when that half of the planet is at its greatest tilt away from the sun, so the sun's rays strike it less directly, the days are shorter, and temperatures are cooler.

Wisdom The ability to judge what is right or true. Wisdom often develops with age and life experience.

Index